UNIVERSITY OF MINNESOTA

⌐ *Emily Dickinson*

BY DENIS DONOGHUE

UNIVERSITY OF MINNESOTA PRESS • MINNEAPOLIS

EMILY DICKINSON

DENIS DONOGHUE is professor of modern English and American literature at University College, Dublin. He is the author of a number of books, including *Jonathan Swift*, *The Ordinary Universe*, *The Third Voice*, and *Connoisseurs of Chaos*.

⤻ *Emily Dickinson*

O<small>N</small> T<small>UESDAY</small>, August 16, 1870, Thomas Wentworth Higginson visited Emily Dickinson at her home in Amherst, Massachusetts. It was their first meeting, although they had been in correspondence since April 1862 when the poet addressed herself to the well-known critic "to say if my Verse is alive." Higginson's account of this first meeting is given in a letter to his wife. "A step like a pattering child's in entry," he reported, "& in glided a little plain woman with two smooth bands of reddish hair & a face a little like Belle Dove's; not plainer — with no good feature — in a very plain & exquisitely clean white pique & a blue net worsted shawl. She came to me with two day lilies which she put in a sort of childlike way into my hand & said 'These are my introduction' in a soft frightened breathless childlike voice — & added under her breath Forgive me if I am frightened; I never see strangers & hardly know what I say . . ." Perhaps Emily Dickinson protested her shyness too much. When she chose to speak, she had no difficulty in finding voice. On this occasion, indeed, "she talked soon & thenceforward continuously — & deferentially — sometimes stopping to ask me to talk instead of her — but readily recommencing." Higginson thought some parts of the conversation worth quoting. "If I read a book," Emily Dickinson said, and if "it makes my whole body so cold no fire ever can warm me I know *that* is poetry. If I feel physically as if the top of my head were taken off, I know *that* is poetry." She spoke of finding "ecstasy in living." When Higginson asked "if she never felt want of employment, never going off the place & never seeing any visitor," she answered, "I never thought of conceiving that I could ever have the slightest approach to such a want in all future time," adding, "I feel that I have not expressed myself strongly enough." In Emily Dickinson the tokens of frailty are genuine, but they do not deny a certain independence of spirit.

Emily Elizabeth Dickinson was born in Amherst on December 10, 1830, the second child of Edward and Emily Dickinson. Her brother William Austin Dickinson was born on April 16, 1829, her sister Lavinia Norcross Dickinson on February 28, 1833. The Dickinsons were an important family in Amherst. Emily's father was a prominent man in public life, treasurer of Amherst College from 1835, a member of the state legislature for several terms, a member of Congress for one term. He was a dedicated Whig, and a resolute defender of temperance. As a parent, he was somewhat harsh, or at best remote: "thin dry & speechless," he appeared to Higginson; "I saw what her life has been." Emily Dickinson told Higginson, "My father only reads on Sunday — he reads *lonely* & *rigorous* books." " 'I say unto you,' Father would read at Prayers, with a militant Accent that would startle one." "Could you tell me what home is," Emily Dickinson asked Higginson; "I never had a mother. I suppose a mother is one to whom you hurry when you are troubled." In 1862 she wrote, "I have a Brother and Sister — My Mother does not care for thought — and Father, too busy with his Briefs — to notice what we do — He buys me many Books — but begs me not to read them — because he fears they joggle the Mind." When her father died, however, in June 1874, Emily was deeply distressed: "Though it is many nights, my mind never comes home." A year later, her mother suffered paralysis and became an invalid for the rest of her life. During those years Emily attended her mother and came to love her. "We were never intimate Mother and Children while she was our Mother — but Mines in the same Ground meet by tunneling and when she became our Child, the Affection came." Mrs. Dickinson died in November 1882: "We hope that Our Sparrow has ceased to fall, though at first we believe nothing."

But "Childhood's citadel" was a somber place. The three children were devoted to one another, but their home did not provoke gaiety. When Austin Dickinson married Susan Gilbert in 1856 and set up house next door, gaiety began to find its natural home. One visitor, Kate Anthon, later recalled happy days to Susan. "Those happy visits at your house! Those celestial evenings in the Library — The blazing *wood* fire — Emily — Austin, — The music — The rampant fun — The inextinguishable laughter, The uproarious spirits of our chosen — our most congenial circle." But that was next door. Edward Dickinson's house was an upright place, indeed perpendicular, in some respects like Mr. Wentworth's house in Henry James's *The Europeans*, where responsibilities are taken hard. "Where are our moral grounds?" Mr. Wentworth demands on an occasion of great stress in that novel, challenged by moral ambiguities painfully French. Emily Dickinson read the novel and quoted Mr. Wentworth's question in a letter to her friend Mrs. Holland. There is a certain propriety in the question, as Emily Dickinson recalled it, since she herself grew up in a place and time of such questions. To her, in that setting, conscience was "Childhood's nurse." Father might be remote, but he was an inescapable moral fact, God but more than God. "I see — New Englandly," Emily Dickinson said in a poem (numbered 285 in the Johnson edition; the numbers in parentheses hereafter refer to that edition). She sees New Englandly for the same reason that, in the same poem, she takes the robin as her "Criterion for Tune," because "I grow — where Robins do."

She went to school at Amherst Academy, studying Latin, French, history, rhetoric, botany, geology, and mental philosophy. In 1847 she entered Mount Holyoke Female Seminary at South Hadley, a lively school where she confronted the large religious questions and engaged in the more tangible study of history, chemistry, Latin, physiology, and English grammar. But her official education was often interrupted by debility and poor health. With the exception of brief visits to Boston, Philadelphia, and Washington, her life was lived entirely in a small New England circle of which Amherst was the center. Even in Amherst her life was not omnivorous. In October 1856 she won the second prize and 75 cents for her rye and Indian bread at the local cattle show, and the following year she was a member of the committee in that category. But she did not roam the hills; she saw what could be seen from her window, from her garden, from next door, occasionally from the church. She chose to live in that way, as if to do so were then to live New Englandly. There is no reason to assume that her choice was morbid. Rather, it was conscientious.

In 1881 she wrote to Higginson. "We dwell as when you saw us — the mighty dying of my Father made no external change — Mother and Sister are with me, and my Brother and pseudo Sister, in the nearest House — When Father lived I remained with him because he would miss me — Now, Mother is helpless — a holier demand — I do not go away, but the Grounds are ample — almost travel — to me, and the few that I knew — came — since my Father died." As a young girl she took her seclusion more lightly. From Mount Holyoke she wrote to her brother, asking, "Has the Mexican war terminated yet & how? Are we beat? Do you know of any nation about to besiege South Hadley?" Years later, she told Mrs. Holland that her notion of politics was accurately represented by the sentence "George Washington was the Father of his Country," qualified by the rejoinder "George Who?" But in fact she kept up with current events, mainly because of her devotion to the *Springfield Daily Republican*. A letter to Susan in September 1882 makes a literary joke of the capture of Ahmed Arabi Pasha at Tel-el-Kebir. Gordon and the British garrison at

Khartoum are fodder for a witty letter to Theodore Holland in 1884. True, she was not interested in "the stale inflation of the minor News." She was odd, reticent, private. In Amherst she was considered a mythological being. Children longed to see her, since the sight would constitute a vision. When the doorbell rang, she ran away, deeper into the house. "All men say 'What' to me," she told Higginson; so she restricted the number of questioners.

If she was a lonely girl, by common standards, loneliness was her choice. Company did not flee her. Some requirement of her sensibility was fulfilled by seclusion which could not have been fulfilled by company. It is clear in the poems that loneliness was one of the conditions she chose to know. Sometimes she thought of isolation as her fate, "circumstance of Lot" (1116), and in the love poems absence of the beloved constitutes a terrible kind of loneliness, "The Horror not to be surveyed" (777). But in one poem (1695) she speaks of "That polar privacy/ A soul admitted to itself," calling it "Finite Infinity." This was the solitude she chose to know; it was like the solitudes of space, sea, and death, but greater than these, because deeper. It occupied a "profounder site" than any other solitude. It is evoked again in another poem (1116) as "another Loneliness/ That many die without." This loneliness is the consequence of "nature," sometimes, and sometimes of "thought," "And whoso it befall/ Is richer than could be revealed/ By mortal numeral." Emily Dickinson elected to be "rich" in this sense, at whatever common cost. Higginson said that the Dickinson home in Amherst was "a house where each member runs his or her own selves." This was especially true of Emily Dickinson's life; she ran her own life, she conducted her own "self." Her sufferings were of the common kind, abrasions of feeling, the pain of loss, partings, deaths; the experiences were not extraordinary, only the particular character of their reception. Loneliness was one of those experiences, remarkable only in the intensity of its reception. It might almost be said that Emily Dickinson did not suffer loneliness; she commanded it. She commanded everything she needed. When she needed a relationship, she commanded it.

The pattern of these relationships is exemplified in Emily Dickinson's friendship with Benjamin Franklin Newton, a law student who spent two years in her father's office in Amherst. Newton was nine years older than Emily Dickinson; he "became to me," she said, "a gentle, yet grave Preceptor, teaching me what to read, what authors to admire, what was most grand or beautiful in nature, and that sublimer lesson, a faith in things unseen, and in a life again, nobler, and much more blessed." He died on March 24, 1853. "When a little Girl, I had a friend," Emily Dickinson later wrote to Higginson, "who taught me Immortality — but venturing too near, himself — he never returned." For the rest of her life, Emily Dickinson sought gentle yet grave preceptors, men older than herself, more accomplished in the ways of the world. It may be said that she sought a father, a more benign father than her own. But this does not say much. The men she found were diverse in character and temper; further differences were prescribed in the terms of each relationship. Rev. Charles Wadsworth was Emily Dickinson's spiritual preceptor for several years. Samuel Bowles, editor of the *Springfield Daily Republican*, was important as an object of feeling: "We miss your vivid Face and the besetting Accents, you bring from your Numidian Haunts." Higginson was Emily Dickinson's literary guide, critic, surgeon. "And for this, Preceptor, I shall bring you — Obedience — the Blossom from my Garden, and every gratitude I know." Her most impassioned relationship was with Judge Otis P. Lord: it appears that Emily Dickinson was in love with him for the last six years of his life, from 1878 to 1884. And there is the unknown man, unless he is Bowles, addressed as "Master": "I want to see you more —

Sir — than all I wish for in this world — and the wish — altered a little — will be my only one — for the skies."

These relationships were important to Emily Dickinson, in different ways and in different degrees. It is impossible to be precise; not enough is known. Where a friendship was crucial to her, she commanded it even beyond the grave, writing to Bowles's widow, for instance, as if to retain the affection by reciting it. Some of her greatest poems were provoked by moments in the drama of these relationships. "He fumbles at your Soul" (315) may be a poem about God, or about some less celestial power; whatever its ostensible subject, it is totally dependent upon the experience of one soul "mastering" another. That experience may be real, or imaginatively conceived; but that it came, however deviously, from Emily Dickinson's sense of master and pupil, there can be no doubt. The least that may be said of these relationships is that they tested, extended, and sometimes tormented her sensibility, with results good in the poems if hard in the life.

Some of the relationships were easy enough. Higginson never quite decided whether his Amherst correspondent was a genius or merely crazed, but it is clear that, within his limits, he helped her. He thought her poems wayward and disorderly, he protested that he could not understand. She promised to do better, next time. But there is no evidence that he damaged the work or disabled the genius. When he published, with Mabel Loomis Todd, Emily Dickinson's *Poems*, the second series, in 1891, one of the first readers was Alice James, sister of Henry James and William James. In her *Diary* for January 6, 1892, she wrote: "It is reassuring to hear the English pronouncement that Emily Dickinson is fifth-rate — they have such a capacity for missing quality; the robust evades them equally with the subtle." Then she continued: "Her being sicklied o'er with T. W. Higginson makes one quake lest there be a latent flaw which escapes one's vision." There were, indeed, latent flaws in Emily Dickinson: a tendency to play up problems as if they were mysteries, a disposition to cultivate the breathless note, a certain coyness disfiguring the charm. But there are no grounds for assuming that Higginson was responsible for these flaws; they were in Emily Dickinson long before she knew her mentor. He is blameless. If he had understood her more profoundly, he would have been, in addition, angelic.

So Emily Dickinson ran her life at Amherst, moving between the kitchen, the garden, her room. She baked bread, made puddings, attended to her knitting, sent messages next door, wrote hundreds of poems and hundreds of letters as pointed as poems. She played the piano. In the garden she had green fingers, succeeding where others failed with Daphne odora, violet, and the day lily. She walked with her dog Carlo, "large as myself, that my Father bought me." From her window, she saw the circus pass. "I saw the sunrise on the Alps since I saw you," she wrote to Mrs. Holland. "Travel why to Nature, when she dwells with us? Those who lift their hats shall see her, as devout do God." Her dreams were bountiful, as in a poem (646) she invoked "Certainties of Sun" and "Midsummer — in the Mind." In the same mood she identified Nature with "what we know," in her own case with the hill, the afternoon, the squirrel, the bumble bee, the bobolink, thunder, the cricket — the unquestionable things. "Nature — the Gentlest Mother is,/ Impatient of no Child" (790). But there were other moods; as Emerson wrote in the essay "Circles," our moods do not believe in each other. In one of those moods (364) nature seemed to Emily Dickinson rude, uttering jubilee the morning after woe; and in another (1624) "an Approving God" sets his minions to work, making pain, sorrow, and death. There is no contradiction. Emily Dickinson is a moody poet, giving herself to the moment.

Perhaps she trusted that, at some level, everything would cohere; one moment would not disown another. "All her life," R. P. Blackmur wrote of her, "she was looking for a subject, and the looking *was* her subject, in life as in poetry." Perhaps she knew this, or hoped against hope that it might be so. In a blunt paraphrase, many of her poems would contradict one another; but her answers are always provisional. Only her questions are definitive. She spent, but did not waste or consume, her life in looking for a subject. Looking for one thing, she nevertheless lived by taking whatever each occasion offered; if it was not the definitive thing, it would serve, for the present, instead of finality. "Forever — is composed of Nows" (624). So she trusted in the significance of Now, and in the search conducted under present auspices. Many poems speak of the "exultation" of search, the thrill of voyaging, "the going/ Of an inland soul to sea" (76). "Our lives are Swiss" (80), she says, except that the imagination discloses to us the Alps and Italy beyond. Let us say that her imagination was Alpine, ascribing to the poet a corresponding urge to scale the heights of experience. "I would go, to know!" (114). In a letter to Higginson she wrote, "Nature is a Haunted House — but Art — a House that tries to be haunted." This does not demean art; rather, it gives the terms of its challenge. To Emily Dickinson, art is the place of experiment and risk, to write is to dare, the imagination sends up strange words as trial balloons. The greatest risks are taken by the inland soul. "To fight aloud, is very brave," she concedes. "But *gallanter*, I know/ Who charge within the bosom/ The Cavalry of Wo" (126). For ignorance, there is nothing to be said. "At least, to know the worst, is sweet!" (172). No wonder Emily Dickinson was content to stay in her room, her garden; with an imagination as challenging as hers, practical experience was bound to appear dull, predictable, banal. She was already far beyond anything life could give as event or experience, because she had already imagined it. She had haunted every house.

13

This was her way. She tested everything, whether it was given by experience or by imagination. Every house had to be searched for ghosts. Many of her poems apply to the great religious doctrines the same interrogative pressure. Of her own religious faith, virtually anything may be said, with some show of evidence. She may be represented as an agnostic, a heretic, a skeptic, a Christian. She grew up in a Christian family, but she was not devout. She did not possess a talent for conviction. In 1873 her father, his own faith recently renewed, arranged that the local Congregational minister, J. L. Jenkins, would offer Emily some spiritual guidance. The interview took place. The minister's son later wrote, "All that is really known is that my father reported to the perplexed parent that Miss Emily was 'sound,' and let it go at that." The report was generous. At about the same time as her spiritual interview, Emily Dickinson wrote to her cousins Louise and Frances Norcross: "There is that which is called an 'awakening' in the church, and I know of no choicer ecstasy than to see Mrs. [Sweetser] roll out in crape every morning, I suppose to intimidate antichrist; at least it would have that effect on me." But, in fact, Emily Dickinson's Christianity was never a firm conviction. As a schoolgirl, she resisted the religious stirrings of her circle; the Amherst revival in 1844 did not succeed with her. In January 1846 she reported to a former schoolmate, Abiah Root, "I was almost persuaded to be a christian," but the strongest word was "almost."

Throughout her life, there were moments in which she longed for faith. In a late poem she wrote:

> Those — dying then,
> Knew where they went —
> They went to God's Right Hand —
> That Hand is amputated now
> And God cannot be found —
>
> The abdication of Belief
> Makes the Behavior small —

> Better an ignis fatuus
> Than no illume at all —   (1551)

But this was one moment among many different moments. Emily
Dickinson seems to have thought of religious faith as an enforced
choice: one must choose between God and man, between eternity
and time. In 1846 she wrote: "I have perfect confidence in God &
his promises & yet I know not why, I feel that the world
holds a predominant place in my affections." The question of
faith was the question of affection, and in the Calvinist idiom one
affection canceled another. In 1848 she wrote: "There is a great
deal of religious interest here and many are flocking to the ark of
safety. I have not yet given up to the claims of Christ, but trust I
am not entirely thoughtless on so important & serious a subject."
But within a short time, she declared herself "standing alone in
rebellion, and growing very careless." She quarreled with Susan
about religion: "and though in that last day, the Jesus Christ you
love, remark he does not know me — there is a darker spirit will
not disown it's child." Again, it is momentary bravado, one rhetoric incited by another. A more urbane version appears some
months later: "I went to church all day in second dress, and boots.
We had such precious sermons from Mr Dwight. One about unbelief, and another Esau. Sermons on unbelief ever did attract me."
Sermons on Christian doctrine did not attract her. When Mr.
Steele preached upon "predestination," she refused to listen; "I
do not respect 'doctrines.' " She wrote to Higginson of her family:
"They are religious — except me — and address an Eclipse, every
morning — whom they call their 'Father.' "
    While Emily Dickinson's early emotions often took a religious
turn, she was never willing to have them curbed by the discipline
of belief. Doctrine was discipline, and therefore alien to a sensibility always somewhat willful. She would have believed, if she had
been allowed to believe anything she liked. In later years her

emotions took several different turns, as if her will were the wind. Now, for the most part, she was content to think of the "Super-natural" as "the Natural, disclosed." Of course, many of her pro-nouncements upon first and last things are more occasional than definitive. She was sincere, but her idea of sincerity was to say whatever, on the given occasion, would help. One of her poems, "How brittle are the Piers" (1433), urges that we may still believe in God and His promises, the evidence being Christ's word. But the poem was enclosed in a letter to Higginson, consoling him after the death of his wife. Another occasion supplied another need, perhaps a different note of consolation; as she wrote, again to Higginson, "To be human is more than to be divine, for when Christ was divine, he was uncontented till he had been human." Reading *Middlemarch*, she was convinced that "the mysteries of human nature surpass the 'mysteries of redemption,' for the in-finite we only suppose, while we see the finite." When a neighbor, Mrs. Stearns, called to inquire if the Dickinsons did not think it shocking for Benjamin Butler to "liken himself to his Redeemer," Emily's answer was "we thought Darwin had thrown 'the Re-deemer' away." But in one of her most ardent letters to Judge Lord, Emily Dickinson, reciting a high ethic, ascribed it to God: "The 'Stile' is God's — My Sweet One — for your great sake — not mine — I will not let you cross — but it is all your's, and when it is right I will lift the Bars." In the same letter: "It may surprise you I speak of God — I know him but a little, but Cupid taught Jehovah to many an untutored Mind — Witchcraft is wiser than we."

Again it is fair to say that Emily Dickinson would have been a Christian if she had been permitted to ascribe to Christ the same status which she ascribed, in that ardent moment, to Cupid and Jehovah; the same, but no more. Clearly, that Christianity would have been merely a function of self, Emily Dickinson's aspiration in one of her many moods. Indeed, it is arguable that religion

was never more to her than a book of metaphors. She did not believe in a Mosaic religion, though the figure of Moses was especially vivid to her. What she wanted, when she wanted anything
in this way, was an Orphic religion, in which dogma and doctrines
would penetrate her sensibility, like music. Truth would suggest
itself as harmony, unassertive because unquestionable, audible
to instinct. "Orpheus' Sermon captivated —/ It did not condemn"
(1545). But to be entranced by Orpheus' song was one thing; to
follow Christ, obeying his word, was another. Christianity offered
itself as truth, embodied with whatever degree of divergence in
doctrine, but it had to reckon with Emily Dickinson's sensibility.
It was the mark of that sensibility either to discard what was offered or to translate it, imperiously, into her own terms.

So she took her Christianity not as she found it but as she altered
it. She read her Bible as a rhetorical manual. Her poems and letters are full of references to Genesis, Revelation, the Psalms, and
the Gospels, but the references are invariably rhetorical. Nothing
is necessarily to be believed, only entertained as a trope. There
are several poems in which Gabriel is invoked, but Emily Dickinson's Gabriel is merely an idealized version of Samuel Bowles or
another wise preceptor, bringing glad tidings and praise. "Get
Gabriel — to tell — the royal syllable" (195); but the syllable in
question is part of the earthly lover's vocabulary. In "The face I
carry with me — last" (336) Gabriel is again assimilated to an
earthly function, endorsing the idiom of love and compliment.
In "Where Thou art — that — is Home" (725) Emily Dickinson is
featured as Mary in Gabriel's praise, but the purpose is hyperbole;
the sacred moment is invoked only to be transcended by the
earthly love declared. In a love letter to Judge Lord she writes,
"Dont you know you have taken my will away and I 'know not
where' you 'have laid' it?"; Mary Magdalene's words give the lover's
complaint its appropriate style.

Emily Dickinson used her hymnbooks in the same way. They are metaphorical and tropical. She owned three hymnbooks: *The Psalms, Hymns, and Spiritual Songs of the Rev. Isaac Watts,* edited by Samuel Worcester; *Church Psalmody, Selected from Dr. Watts and Other Authors,* edited by Lowell Mason and David Greene; and *Village Hymns, a Supplement to Dr. Watts's Psalms and Hymns,* edited by Asahel Nettleton. The letters and poems often depend upon the recollection of a hymn or of phrases from a hymn. A letter of September 1877 to Mrs. Holland recalls, somewhat loosely, a phrase from Watts's hymn "Were the Whole Realm of Nature Mine." But again the hymn is recalled for the phrase. "How precious Thought and Speech are! 'A present so divine,' was in a Hymn they used to sing when I went to Church." For Emily Dickinson, the estate of the hymns is ablative; rhythms and phrases are retained, but not their endorsing faith. What she took from the hymns, beyond that need, was a prosody; like other English and American poets she wrote secular poems in the meters of the Psalms, particularly the common measure.

The pattern persists in her reading. She took what her sensibility needed, from whatever source. Her motive in reading other writers, great and small, was not to discover the variety and potentiality of the art she shared with them, but rather to find there a provocation for her own imagination. Sometimes a phrase was enough. She was deeply engaged by the Brontës, but on the other hand the abiding interest of Emily Brontë largely resolved itself in a magical line, "Every existence would exist in Thee," from "No Coward Soul Is Mine." The line is quoted three times in letters. A few writers were deeply pondered. "After long disuse of her eyes," Higginson said, "she read Shakespeare & thought why is any other book needed." But even with Shakespeare her needs were exclusive. Sometimes a line moved her because of its associations: " 'An envious Sliver broke' was a passage your Uncle peculiarly loved in the drowning Ophelia," she told Abbie Farley, niece of Judge Lord. The same phrase occurs in a letter, nearly five years earlier, to Mrs. Holland. The reading of Longfellow's *Kavanagh* caused a domestic flurry, so it lodged inordinately in her imagination. Reading novels, she often compared the relationships with her own, playing personal games with *David Copperfield* and *The Old Curiosity Shop*. She read the American writers, notably Bryant, Emerson, Hawthorne, and Lowell, when their current work appeared in the *Atlantic Monthly* or when it was announced in a current periodical, *Scribner's Monthly* or another. She was assiduous in reading Higginson. Often, as in that case, her interest in the work was primarily an interest in the writer. She was enchanted by the Brownings, Elizabeth "that Foreign Lady" and Robert "the consummate Browning." She read virtually everything by George Eliot, and admired her greatly, but she never chose to say anything of critical significance about the works, except that *Daniel Deronda* was a "wise and tender Book." But she was fascinated by the news of George Eliot's life, and pursued every biographical detail. When she read of the novelist's death, she wrote to the Norcrosses: "The look of the words as they lay in the print I shall never forget. Not their face in the casket could have had the eternity to me. Now, *my* George Eliot." Clearly, Emily Dickinson's interest in George Eliot as a romantic and heroic figure transcended her critical concern with the novels; she was moved by George Eliot's representative character, the aura surrounding her. The books merely provided evidence that the personal interest was not grossly misplaced.

This may help to explain the vagaries of Emily Dickinson's literary taste. Sometimes the explanation is simple; if a writer reached her under Higginson's auspices, he was sure of approval. There were exceptions. Higginson appears to have suggested that she read Joaquin Miller's *Songs of the Sierras*, but she declined.

"I did not read Mr Miller because I could not care about him — Transport is not urged." On the other hand she read Helen Hunt Jackson's poems, recommended by Higginson, and echoed his praise. "Mrs Hunt's Poems are stronger than any written by Women since Mrs — Browning, with the exception of Mrs Lewes." Later, she went further. When Higginson's *Short Studies of American Authors* appeared in 1879, she wrote to him: "Mrs Jackson soars to your estimate lawfully as a Bird, but of Howells and James, one hesitates — Your relentless Music dooms as it redeems." But the real difference between Mrs. Jackson and her male competitors was that Emily Dickinson had already met and approved the authoress; she never met James or Howells. Her critical standards were largely determined by the local requirements of her sensibility. A multitude of poetic defects might readily be covered by her friendship and affection. In any case, her reading was casual. Books came to her, and she read them, but she never allowed her mind to be intimidated by anything she read. Indeed, she was easily put off by a personal consideration. It is not certain that she ever read Poe: "Of Poe, I know too little to think." "You speak of Mr Whitman," she wrote to Higginson; "I never read his Book — but was told that he was disgraceful."

That her sensibility was strange is clear enough. It often appears, in the relation between her imagination and reality, that very little reality was required, her imagination being what it was, exorbitantly acute. Reading her poems, one is surprised to find that they have any base in reality or fact, since a base in that element is what they seem least to need. Philosophers have sometimes wondered what would happen if our senses were to be, for some inordinate reason, acutely intensified, the first conclusion being that the victim would inhabit a different universe of relationships. There is a passage in *Middlemarch* (Chapter XX) where George Eliot considers how little reality the human frame can bear.

"If we had a keen vision and feeling of all ordinary human life," she says, "it would be like hearing the grass grow and the squirrel's heart beat, and we should die of that roar which lies on the other side of silence." It often seems as if Emily Dickinson's senses were of this order. But there is a difference. The sensory power, as George Eliot conceives it, is still a power of response to reality, and it serves reality as its first and last object. It claims nothing for itself; it is willing to lose itself in the grass of ordinary human life. But the intensity of Emily Dickinson's imagination has a different object. She is not, after all, one of the great celebrants of life, the proof being how little of life, in the common sense, she chose to live. It is the peculiar nature of her sensibility that it deals with experience by exacerbating it, as if prompted by a conscience for which nothing less would do. No wonder she restricted the amount of life she was prepared to live, since the living had to be so intense, so relentlessly acute.

Santayana has written of the "Poetry of Barbarism," meaning in the given cases Browning and Whitman; in general, the barbarian "is the man who regards his passions as their own excuse for being." So far as this goes, Emily Dickinson is a barbarian, and her barbarism arises from the same source, the rejection of classic and Christian ideals of discipline. But there is a crucial distinction. To Emily Dickinson, the passions required no excuse because they were the life and form of her sensibility; and sensibility was one guise of her conscience. In this way and from this direction, the exercise of sensibility became the exercise of conscience and duty. She saw and heard the grass grow, but she saw and heard New Englandly; so she wore the rue of her barbarism with a difference. This is why she gives the impression, contrasted with Whitman and Browning, of living upon her nerves; in this contrast, Whitman and Browning appear even more nonchalant than they are.

Think, for instance, how she goes out of her way to cultivate what others go out of their way to avoid, the intensities of
apprehension made possible by pain. "A *Wounded* Deer — leaps
highest" (165), so wounds are sought. The "scant degree/ Of Life's
penurious Round" (313) can only be raised by leaps of perception, magic, witchcraft. The leaps are facilitated by "Opposites,"
which therefore "entice" as "Water, is taught by thirst" (135). "I
like a look of Agony," she says, "Because I know it's true" (241).
In a later poem (963) "A nearness to Tremendousness —/ An
Agony procures," and the agony is its own justification. This is, in
other poems, the idiom of awe, an epic grandeur of spirit which
shames the petty difference between happiness and misery. One
of her most powerful poems (281) begins, " 'Tis so appalling — it
exhilirates." This is not a melodramatic indulgence, a self-regard-
ing exercise in Gothic horror; it is, for this New England poet, the
conscientious imagination at its sworn task. Emily Dickinson's
special way of feeling is to drive apprehension to the pitch of awe;
at that pitch, the discrimination of subject and object in the act
of perception is dissolved, and a new state strains to be released.
This is the moment at which "Perception of an object costs/ Precise the Object's loss" (1071). The object does not detach itself
from the subject; rather, the dualism of subject and object is, in a
flash, consumed. What occupies the scene then is a new state of
consciousness. The given object, like experience itself in Emily
Dickinson, must take the risk of losing itself to a new state, becom-
ing something else which is not the sum of experience and sensibility but their product. Consciousness is X, an unknown quantity,
unknown because its limits have never been reached. Free of
limits, it can enter into majestic equations with other quantities,
known by name if not yet measured. In a poem on the free soul
(384) Emily Dickinson says, "Captivity is Consciousness —/ So's
Liberty."

Her word for this unknown quantity, when she does not call it consciousness, is circumference. In one poem (1620) it is "Circumference thou Bride of Awe." In "Circles" Emerson says: "The life of man is a self-evolving circle, which, from a ring imperceptibly small, rushes on all sides outwards to new and larger circles, and that without end." These circles are always deemed to be known, because divinely allowed and consistent with the human mind. The circles, in another version, are concentric, with man at the center, so they can be verified at any moment. But circumference, as Emily Dickinson uses the word, marks an area, on all sides, where consciousness ranges beyond enclosure. It is her version of the sublime. Circles define what they enclose; since an expanding circle depends upon the force of soul, in Emerson's terms, it may be held at any point. But circumference marks the end of definition and the beginning of risk. As Emily Dickinson put it (633), "When Cogs — stop — that's Circumference —/ The Ultimate — of Wheels," using Emerson's words with her own inflection. Another kindred word is impossibility: in one poem (838), "Impossibility, like Wine/ Exhilirates the Man/ Who tastes it; Possibility/ Is flavorless." And there is, in forty poems, immortality; which, nearly enough, is the spiritual form of impossibility. They are all sublime terms, as Emily Dickinson uses them, outrunning nature. "I worried Nature with my Wheels/ When Her's had ceased to run" (786).

But the key word is consciousness. Sometimes it is equated with God. "The Brain — is wider than the Sky"; it is "deeper than the sea." Finally, it is "just the weight of God"; if it differs from God, it is only as "Syllable from Sound" (632). In another poem it is equated with life itself. "No Drug for Consciousness — can be" (786); if this is the form of "Being's Malady," the only escape is to die. The justification of consciousness is the justification of will; given the power, one must use it. "What are the sinews of such cordage for/ Except to bear" (1113). But there is another justification. Samuel Beckett has ascribed to Proust some thoughts on habit. "If Habit is a second nature, it keeps us in ignorance of the first, and is free of its cruelties and its enchantments." To Emily Dickinson, it appears, the common part of experience was a habit. She seems to have thought of religious belief, for instance, as a habit, perhaps a good habit, but open to the same disability, that, congealed as second nature, it prevents us from seeing our first. Institutions were dedicated to the formation of habit. But the chief means of defeating or circumventing habit was the imagination, consciousness. The imagination insists upon penetrating to the cruelties and enchantments of our first nature; that is its particular glory, and from thence it acquires its heroic note. This perhaps explains why Emily Dickinson is constantly forcing her mind beyond or beneath the familiar marks of the senses, the easy gifts. If she sees something, she never rests content with sight or even with possession of what it sees; she always goes further, further back or further forward, in her own directions. Very often her mind, in a typical cadence, starts with the sense, or with the declared failure of sense, only to run from it, above or below:

> Not seeing, still we know —
> Not knowing, guess —
> Not guessing, smile and hide
> And half caress —
>
> And quake — and turn away . . .　(1518)

Or, more urbanely: "To see is perhaps never quite the sorcery that it is to surmise, though the obligation to enchantment is always binding." It is as if the senses themselves, for all their merit, merely beguiled one into habit, and something else was needed, a sixth sense, critical and subversive, to correct the happy five. The sixth sense is the imagination.

There is another way of putting it. In the Preface to *The Por*-

trait of a Lady Henry James, explaining the special light in which he saw his heroine Isabel Archer, says that he conceived of the center of the subject as Isabel's consciousness, with one particular qualification. Shakespeare's heroines, George Eliot's heroines, are mainly revealed in their relations to other characters. Isabel Archer is mainly revealed in her relation to herself. This is, preeminently, the main direction of her consciousness. We think of Emily Dickinson in this character, without forcing the comparison. Emily's relations to other people were sufficiently numerous and sufficiently engrossing for her particular purposes, but they were all, in varying measure, as James says of Isabel's relations to other people, "contributive only to the greater one," her relation to herself. Some of Emily Dickinson's most daring poems turn the speaker into a haunted house, where she is at once the house, the ghost, and the haunted inhabitant:

> Ourself behind ourself, concealed —
> Should startle most —
> Assassin hid in our Apartment
> Be Horror's least.   (670)

In another poem, the mind's quarrel with itself is conducted in terms of banishment, monarchy, and abdication:

> But since Myself — assault Me —
> How have I peace
> Except by subjugating
> Consciousness?   (642)

Indeed, when we speak of Emily Dickinson's relation to herself, we should think of it rather as a relation to her many selves, the different ghosts haunting her house.

So the "charm of the actual," which James recites in his *Autobiography*, had to meet, in Emily Dickinson, the resistance of a demanding sensibility. There are several poems in which the charm, like Orpheus, overcomes the resistance, but the defeat of resistance was never final. Emily Dickinson seems to have a scrupulous objection, a qualm of conscience, whenever any charm comes too easily. To lie in Abraham's bosom seems a guilty indulgence. Certainly, her imagination is more often animated by the feeling which flows toward its object, and then flows away, than by the feeling which rests there. There are several poems on expectation, which qualify the common estimate of the relation between expectation and fulfillment. "Expectation — is Contentment —/ Gain — Satiety" (807); the reason is that there must be "an Austere trait in Pleasure." "Danger — deepens Sum," partly because the sense of danger, like fear, may be exhilarating, and partly because, at such moments, the will is exercised. But the will is exercised even more dramatically in Emily Dickinson's afterwords. Indeed, there is a special rhythm in her sensibility which is heard when the chosen estate is ablative.

There is an extraordinary letter to the Norcrosses, August 1876, in which Emily Dickinson speaks of cats, and especially of her sister Vinnie's new cat, "the color of Branwell Brontë's hair." Then she says: "You remember my ideal cat has always a huge rat in its mouth, just going out of sight — though going out of sight in itself has a peculiar charm. It is true that the unknown is the largest need of the intellect, though for it, no one thinks to thank God." But if the unknown has this status among needs of the intellect, equal status must be given to that which has been known and is now gone. To Emily Dickinson, a peculiar charm resides in "going out of sight," when the object, lost or consumed, becomes a part of memory, loss, and need. "By a departing light/ We see acuter, quite,/ Than by a wick that stays" (1714). In Emily Dickinson generally, experiences are more intensely apprehended just after their loss. Wallace Stevens wrote of "credences of Summer," but Emily Dickinson believed in summer more profoundly when it was just gone. "Summer has two Beginnings —/ Beginning once in June —/ Beginning in October/ Affectingly again" (1422). Indeed, she owned an October imagination, with June for experience. To apprehend June in June is of course a joy, called "Riot," but the October sense of June is "graphicer for Grace," presumably because Grace is a mode of the imagination. For the same reason, "finer is a going/ Than a remaining Face"; a remaining face is merely entertained, the other is recovered by a strain of will. "That it will never come again/ Is what makes life so sweet" (1741). This is why Emily Dickinson's imagination so often moves along "a route of evanescence," as if on one side everything were premonition, and on the other the fatality of loss. In one of her most majestic poems, "As imperceptibly as Grief," when the summer has "lapsed away,"

> The Dusk drew earlier in —
> The Morning foreign shone —
> A courteous, yet harrowing Grace,
> As Guest, that would be gone —   (1540)

The morning sunshine is foreign because alien, intractable in its resistance to the rhythm of lapse and departure.

There are many variants in the rhythm of evanescence. Some are easy, like the "dear retrospect" (1742) in which the dead are recalled. When evanescence is positively sought, it is called renunciation, "The letting go/ A Presence — for an Expectation." A few lines later, "Renunciation — is the Choosing/ Against itself —/ Itself to justify/ Unto itself" (745). This is another version of Emily Dickinson's scruple, where evanescence is felt New Englandly. In the love poems, evanescence is absence of the lover, where absence recalls and enforces presence so vividly that both states are transformed to something else, for which the poem is the only name. The transformation is achieved by writing the poem. "To lose thee — sweeter than to gain/ All other hearts I knew" (1754). And there is a consolatory poem, sent to Higginson when Emily Dickinson read of his infant daughter's death: "The Face in evanescence lain/ Is more distinct than our's" (1490). Indeed, it almost appears that Emily Dickinson welcomed pain and loss for the intensity they provoked; or, if that is excessive, that she was extraordinarily resourceful in finding power where common eyes see only pain.

If this sounds somewhat Emersonian, the association may be allowed and pursued. In the fifth chapter of the long essay *Nature*, there is a beautiful passage of evanescence. "When much intercourse with a friend has supplied us with a standard of excellence, and has increased our respect for the resources of God who thus sends a real person to outgo our ideal; when he has, moreover, become an object of thought, and, whilst his character retains all its unconscious effect, is converted in the mind into solid and sweet wisdom, it is a sign to us that his office is closing, and he is commonly withdrawn from our sight in a short time." This goes beyond acceptance to a deep assent, an Emersonian "yea." The equivalent in Emily Dickinson is more resistant, less urbane; or the urbanity may be presumed to reach the words much later. Emerson's posture is one of assent, even before the circumstances arrive to request assent. Emily Dickinson takes up no position at all, makes no promises, until the occasion demands an answer. There is a passage in *The Spoils of Poynton* which is closer to her spirit. In Chapter XXI of James's novel Fleda Vetch goes to visit Mrs. Gereth at her house, Ricks. Fleda is enchanted with the place, and particularly with what Mrs. Gereth has made of it. The house declares a sense of loss, but this is part of its distinction — "the impression somehow of something dreamed and missed, something reduced, relinquished, resigned: the poetry, as it were, of something sensibly *gone*." She conceives of the house as haunted by its characteristic ghosts. Ricks has been owned by Mrs. Gereth's old maiden aunt, to whom Fleda now ascribes "a great accepted pain." This is something like the pain of Emily Dickinson's world, great and accepted but still pain. It is the note of tragedy where Emerson's is the note of romance or, finally, the note of comedy. We hear Emily Dickinson's note in a poem (910) about the incrimination of mind and experience; the discipline of man forces him to choose "His Preappointed Pain."

This is Emily Dickinson's special area of feeling: the preappointed pain, how we choose it, the consequences of the choice. If her poems had titles, the names would fix themselves upon the great abstractions, the large words which range the individual acts and sufferings of man in categories, as pain, love, self, will, desire, expectation, and death. From these grand categories the particular experience issues, moving toward the sensibility; there the drama begins, if it has not already begun in the mind's engagement with itself. For the poem, it does not matter; great poems have been written according to both prescriptions. With Emily Dickinson's poems in view it is only a minor extravagance to say that nearly everything is sensibility. "Tell me what the artist is," James said in the Preface to *The Portrait of a Lady*, "and I will tell you of what he has *been* conscious."

So we come, by a long way round, to the definitive poems; or to a sample, barely enough to suggest what the extraordinary enterprise of Emily Dickinson's vision came to.

> After great pain, a formal feeling comes —
> The Nerves sit ceremonious, like Tombs —
> The stiff Heart questions was it He, that bore,
> And Yesterday, or Centuries before?
>
> The Feet, mechanical, go round —
> Of Ground, or Air, or Ought —
> A Wooden way
> Regardless grown,
> A Quartz contentment, like a stone —
>
> This is the Hour of Lead —
> Remembered, if outlived,

> As Freezing persons, recollect the Snow —
> First — Chill — then Stupor — then the letting go —   (341)

In a letter to Higginson, April 25, 1862, Emily Dickinson wrote: "I had a terror — since September — I could tell to none — and so I sing, as the Boy does by the Burying Ground — because I am afraid." It is agreed that this poem issued from the September terror, whatever other form that terror took, including "a funeral in my brain" (280). But the reverberation of the poem comes not from one historical crisis but from a classic situation, "felt in the blood" and exacerbated till it released itself in this form. The situation, as given in another poem (396), is "Pain's Successor — When the Soul/Has suffered all it can." So the poem is a ritual, imaginatively conducted from the great accepted pain to the "letting go." But the ritual has been practiced in many other poems, which we may call afterpoems to indicate a characteristic figure already glossed. Indeed, it may have been necessary for Emily Dickinson to practice her ritual in twenty more or less preparatory poems, all devoted to the same figure, so that she might employ the ritual in this great poem once for all.

The poem allows the experience whatever latitude it needs to impose its own nature, as the nerves, the heart, and the feet maintain the disjunct semblance of life, everything but its animating principle — the formula, without the spiritual form. This is what experience brings to sensibility. What sensibility has done to the experience is exacerbation, but in a peculiar kind. The experience is all intensity, and in an exactly equal and opposite measure the sensibility is all resistance. Discipline is the enabling form of resistance, in this poem and for this occasion. What seems like numbness in the poem is ostensible; it is really the effect of resistance offered by sensibility to the experience. Set off against the terror and the pain there are the strict sentences, severe, formal, ascetic. That is to say, the sensibility is operative pre-eminently in the syntax. The wilder the experience, the more decorous the sentence. In another poem (735), giving the same principle, Emily Dickinson speaks of "Life's sweet Calculations" imposed upon "Concluded Lives"; music played at a funeral "Makes Lacerating Tune": "To Ears the Dying Side —/ 'Tis Coronal — and Funeral —/ Saluting — in the Road."

Of the demanding passions in Emily Dickinson, the first is love. "Till it has loved — no man or woman can become itself — Of our first Creation we are unconscious," she wrote to Higginson. Is there more than love and death, she asked Mrs. Holland. It often seems as if, for the good of her poems, nothing more was required. "I cannot live with You" (640) is one of her grand love poems, one to remind the reader of many; and "Unable are the Loved to die" (809) will serve to hold the two motifs together, as they so often come together in this poet. "Born — Bridalled — Shrouded —/ In a Day," she exclaims in a famous poem (1072). The love lyrics, naturally enough, are subject to exacerbation. If she writes of desire, there is the demand for fulfillment, but the demand is hardly spoken until it is almost retracted, "lest the Actual —/ Should disenthrall thy soul" (1430), a characteristic sequence. Do not, she says in another poem (1434), try to "climb the Bars of Ecstasy," since "In insecurity to lie/ Is Joy's insuring quality." Love, indeed, is one of the two great absolutes in Emily Dickinson's world, the other being death. Many of her poems enact certain moments on the way toward love, including desire, expectation, premonition, fear. But more poems still dispose certain moments on the other side of love, as loss, despair, terror, then death.

For despair, there are several poems, and those among her finest achievements. In "There's a certain Slant of light" (258) despair is absolute, beyond question or argument:

> There's a certain Slant of light,
> Winter Afternoons —

> That oppresses, like the Heft
> Of Cathedral Tunes —

Heft means weight, with a further note of heaving, strain, oppression. The cathedral tunes oppress because of the sullen weight of faith which they ask the listener to receive and to lift. These intimations course back through "oppresses" to the slant of light, which would be neutral and innocent, even with the addition of winter afternoons. This is one of Emily Dickinson's common procedures, to start a poem with a first line which is neutral, or as neutral as the barest narrative can be; and then to expose the line to alien associations, until it, too, is tainted and there is nothing but the alien. On the face of it, the slant of light is innocent, but its innocence cannot survive the accretion of oppressive effects. The sinister element is not visible, in the nature of the case cannot be visible, light being merely light; so the sinister element is within. By the beginning of the second stanza, the light brings "Heavenly Hurt," again invisible, making only an internal difference, "Where the Meanings, are." Now its absolute nature appears, alien like the cathedral tunes, an absolute music, malign and in that nature heavenly. Emily Dickinson now gathers these intimations together, calling them despair, "An imperial affliction/ Sent us of the air"; so the air, too, like the wintry light, is tainted, slave of Heaven:

> When it comes, the Landscape listens —
> Shadows — hold their breath —
> When it goes, 'tis like the Distance
> On the look of Death —

It is as if the landscape were on the poet's side, sharing the terror; there is enmity even between the light and nature, alien premonitions. But the poet does not call upon the landscape to receive her, hiding her feeling from the light. She merely notes a further enmity, another figure, oppressed in its own way. Perhaps the distance between the poet and her landscape is narrowed somewhat by the shadows; but again there is no kinship. When the despair goes, it leaves behind not its opposite but a memory of itself, looking now like the face of death. Distance and death are cousins in many of Emily Dickinson's poems, especially in the love poems, where the absence of the lover, his distance, is indeed like death. Here the despair has defined its "seal" or sign as the personification of death; when the seal is defined in this final sense, the poem is finished.

The same association of despair merging in death is made in another poem (305):

> The difference between Despair
> And Fear — is like the One
> Between the instant of a Wreck —
> And when the Wreck has been —

Fear is not further described, it is absolute in its way. But despair is given as an image in the second and last stanza; it is transformed to death:

> The Mind is smooth — no Motion —
> Contented as the Eye
> Upon the Forehead of a Bust
> That knows — it cannot see —

It is a quartz contentment. Emily Dickinson often uses words like "contented" and "content" in a special sense. When something is, once for all, what it is, when it is the "perfection" of itself, with all its possibilities embodied in one figure, it may be fancied to be content, whatever its nature or character. Good or bad is indifferent. If one is thinking of existence, merely, then all things which equally exist are equal. In another poem (756) she describes an inordinate blessing she had, "A perfect — paralyzing Bliss," definitive, ultimate. Then she says, "Contented as Despair," meaning that both the bliss and the despair were absolute. They may decorously be compared with each other, or with anything else similarly perfect. This is one of the marks of Emily Dickinson's sensibility, that it takes particular note of a thing's perfection, whatever its nature; takes note, and allows to the perfection of pain the same credence as to the perfection of joy. Both are definitive, therefore contented. In Emily Dickinson, everything is allowed to become itself, whatever the character of that self; it will not be deprived of its possibilities. This is why we think of her as preeminently associated not with pain, joy, or loneliness, but with accepted pain, accepted joy, accepted loneliness. Her ministry does not end with acceptance, but it never begins without acceptance. To accept that something is what it is, and that its character is its own, is the first act of her sensibility. What the later acts are, only the poems can say. "It might be lonelier/ Without the Loneliness" (405), because the loneliness has become a character, almost a person, in Emily Dickinson's life, a member of the house. Darkness and a room have been prepared for his reception; even such a person might be missed. "Not seeing, still we know" (1518), the statues may say; but if all they know is that they cannot see, that is despair, fear's afterword.

It is evident that there is an apocalyptic element in Emily Dickinson's imagination. We think of it when we advert to its rage for completeness, perfection; it insists upon conceiving what lesser imaginations, or more genial imaginations, are content to hint. It forces itself to the end of the line. Mostly, in Emily Dickinson's poems, the end of the line is death; so her imagination insists upon conceiving that, too. There is a passage in one of George Eliot's letters, July 1, 1874: "Your picture of Mr. and Mrs. Stirling, and what you say of the reasons why one may wish even for the anguish of being *left* for the sake of waiting on the beloved one to the end — all that goes to my heart of hearts. It is what I think of almost daily. For death seems to me now a close, real experience, like the approach of autumn or winter, and I am glad to find that advancing life brings this power of imagining the nearness of death I never had till of late years." This is very much in Emily Dickinson's spirit. Among perfections, death is hardly to be challenged. "To be alive — is Power" (677); true enough, and especially true in Emily Dickinson's poems, but if all absolutes are, in this respect, equal, an apocalyptic imagination attends most upon death. Or rather, upon dying, since this slight change in the character of the word makes the conceit more approachable.

A motto for these death poems is provided in a poem (412) in which Emily Dickinson says, "I made my soul familiar — with her extremity —/ That at the last, it should not be a novel Agony." As always, she exacerbates what is domestic, domesticates the apocalypse; either way, the imagination asserts itself. Death and the soul are to be "acquainted —/ Meet tranquilly, as friends," or if not as friends, then as neighbors, to whom courtesy is due. In "The last Night that She lived" (1100) Emily Dickinson notes that "It was a Common Night/ Except the Dying — this to Us/ Made Nature different." The tone is properly judicious; the mourners are, to an unusual degree, aware of things, but we are not to hear the grass grow. Ordinary things are "Italicized — as 'twere." The feelings are ordinary, too, the common resentment that the dead child has been chosen and others less worthy left:

> We waited while She passed —
> It was a narrow time —
> Too jostled were Our Souls to speak . . .

The mourners merely wait while the dying one goes; because the waiting is oppressive, the time is narrow; even in the hours and minutes before the death, friends are already conceived as attending the funeral, sitting around the corpse, congested. The language of soul is taken from the language of body, as the language of eternity is derived from the language of time, because there is no

35

other language. All language is, in this sense, domestic. Death poems are life poems. Emily Dickinson's death poems accept this condition; acceptance gives them their extraordinary resilience. It is as if she had only to assent to the temporal nature of language, cooperating with its domestic bias, to write death poems which are among the greatest short poems in the language. "Too jostled were Our Souls to speak": here the imagination is going about its proper business, not by trying to do the whole work but by co-operating with the language. "Jostled" is the product of a dramatic imagination in league with a domestically inclined language; knowing, too, that what is beyond experience must accept a finite language, or remain silent. At the end of the poem the mourners are released to their own lives: "And then an awful leisure was/ Belief to regulate." To regulate; to govern, direct, or control, a discipline domestic in its language, esoteric in its particular application. The strongest link in Emily Dickinson's chain is invariably the common word, taken from a domestic language and applied, with the force of courtesy, where ostensibly it does not belong. This is why her triumphs so often appear, on first reading, to be wrong; and then we know them to be incalculably right: "I died for Beauty — but was scarce/ Adjusted in the Tomb . . ." (449).

This is to say that Emily Dickinson uses a plebeian language with a patrician imagination; willingly, with the commitment of knowledge. That the words are plebeian has perhaps already appeared; that the imagination is patrician appears in its independence, its pride, its *sprezzatura*. Where both forces are fully engaged, the result is a classic poem, as near perfection as the association allows. "I heard a Fly buzz — when I died" (465) is such an occasion. The speaker is the dying one, the "post of observation" her deathbed. The mourners are given as eyes and breaths, the breaths "gathering firm/ For that last Onset — when the King/ Be witnessed — in the Room." Then the dying one sees a fly interposed "Between the light — and me"; "And then the Windows failed — and then/ I could not see to see." Death is imagined, in the last stanza, as the end of a sequence in which the first parts are played by things not yet to die. In the victim's failing life the buzzing fly is there, but "With Blue — uncertain stumbling Buzz," then the windows fail, two failures prefiguring a third, "I could not see to see." Allen Tate has recalled the last scene in Dostoevski's *The Idiot*, where Prince Myshkin and Rogozhin stand, in the dark, over the corpse of the murdered Nastasya. A fly appears, out of nowhere, and settles upon Nastasya's pillow. Mr. Tate says of the fly that it "comes to stand in its sinister and abundant life for the privation of life, the body of the young woman on the bed." In Emily Dickinson's poem the fly hovers to represent all the remaining things, alien because resistant, which detach themselves from the dying; privation, yes, but perhaps in greater measure, alienation. The imagination, when it is dramatic, seeks to establish relations between perceiver and the thing perceived, as here the dying speaker draws fly and window to herself, to her own lapse and failure. The effort fails when, with death, detachment is complete. There is a passage in Wordsworth's Preface to his *Poems* of 1815 where the poet describes this tendency of the imagination; he speaks of "images independent of each other, and immediately endowed by the mind with properties that do not inhere in them, upon an incitement from properties and qualities the existence of which is inherent and obvious." In Emily Dickinson's poem the imagination, conceiving of the mourners, the fly, the air in the room, and the windows, draws everything into the circle of lapse and failure until the last line, when the center fails, and there is nothing.

For the same reason, in "Because I could not stop for Death" (712) the imagination represents the grain as "Gazing." The gaze is transferred from the speaker; or rather, the speaker draws the

37

grain toward herself, to share in the nature of her vision. Indeed, this imaginative principle is active in the structure of the poem. Grim death is domesticated, fitted to the common sequences of life, a gentleman of Amherst come to call upon a lady. Yeats speaks of "that discourtesy of death," Emily Dickinson enacts its civility. The gentleman caller arrives, and conveys his lady to the carriage. The poem has been compared with Browning's "The Last Ride Together," partly on the strength of Browning's lines —

> What if we still ride on, we two
> With life for ever old yet new,
> Changed not in kind but in degree,
> The instant made eternity . . .

It is a nice conjunction, especially when we recall that Emily Dickinson, reading Browning's poem several years later, was struck by the line "So, one day more am I deified" in the second stanza. But Browning's poem has nothing of Emily Dickinson's civility. A comparison nearer home is feasible, a later poem by Emily Dickinson herself (1445) in which death is personified as "the supple Suitor/ That wins at last"; a comparison the more attractive because both poems stroke death with the melody of love. In the later poem death's "stealthy Wooing" is first conducted by "pallid innuendoes":

> But brave at last with Bugles
> And a bisected Coach
> It bears away in triumph
> To Troth unknown
> And Kinsmen as divulgeless
> As throngs of Down —

It is a different pageantry, of course. The pageantry of "Because I could not stop for Death" is a more equable courtship, featured in the slow drive into the country, the courtesy with which the gentleman pauses so that they may look at the old house. So the conclusion is quieter, there are no bugles:

> Since then — 'tis Centuries — and yet
> Feels shorter than the Day
> I first surmised the Horses Heads
> Were toward Eternity —

Surmise; meaning, to go somewhat beyond the evidence. Evidence gives the direction, but not the distance or the end. It is as if the whole enterprise, death's designs upon the soul, were conducted by "stealthy Wooing," without the bravery of bugles and triumph. In "surmised" one stealth is quietly answered by another.

What is remarkable in the poem is the power of an imagination which can live, apparently, upon so little. We feel that a poem which aspires to do so much might reasonably claim, for its essential materials, pretty nearly everything. But this poem does more with poverty than other poems with wealth; or so it is permissible to feel. A few common words, a simple plot, almost nothing in the way of description, no thoughts, no ideas; and the extraordinary work is done. There is something of this seeming ease in another poem about death (1078), or rather about the morning after a death:

> The Bustle in a House
> The Morning after Death
> Is solemnest of industries
> Enacted upon Earth —
>
> The Sweeping up the Heart
> And putting Love away
> We shall not want to use again
> Until Eternity.

William Dean Howells quoted the last lines in his review of *Poems of Emily Dickinson* in January 1891, and he recalled them, several years later, when he visited his daughter's grave in Boston. "What an indescribable experience!" he wrote to Mark Twain, October 23, 1898; "I thought I could tell you about it, but I can't. Do you know those awful lines of Emily Dickinson?" And he quoted them. Deaths were many in Amherst, as Emily Dickinson's poems and letters show; and, to her, the only really accredited rituals were domestic, the daily industries. It is typical of her imagination to see the solemnity of death yield, as a matter of domestic fact, to the sense of continuing life, while the accepted loss persists. So the domestic rituals are the serious endgames, played when one season yields to another, but there is no attempt to assuage the loss by invoking the rhythms of seasonal time to transcend it. Loss is absolute, too.

In October 1883, Emily Dickinson's nephew Gilbert died, the youngest child of Austin and Susan, eight years old, from typhoid fever. "Dawn and Meridian in one," she wrote to Susan, enclosing an elegy, "Pass to thy Rendezvous of Light,/ Pangless except for us" (1564). To Emily herself, sorrow was inexpressible. Within a few weeks she was ill. "The Physician says I have 'Nervous prostration.' Possibly I have — I do not know the Names of Sickness. The Crisis of the sorrow of so many years is all that tires me." In March 1884, Judge Lord died. "I hardly dare to know that I have lost another friend, but anguish finds it out." In June, she herself suffered a nervous collapse. "I have not been strong for the last year," she told her friend Mrs. Mack; she was never to be strong again. The last letters tell the story, often in single lines. There are occasional spurts of energy, and the result is a longer letter, or a few lines of verse. In August 1885, Helen Jackson died. During the following months Emily Dickinson's letters are necessities of condolence, often picking up fragments of the dead lives and sharing them with friends. Her health improved a little in the spring of 1886: "The velocity of the ill, however, is like that of the snail," she told Charles Clark, Wadsworth's friend. In May, she became ill again. On the thirteenth she passed into a coma, paralysis as a consequence of Bright's disease. She died on Saturday evening, May 15, 1886.

Some time after her death, her sister Lavinia found a locked box containing about seven hundred short poems. The pages were bound together in fascicles of four or five sheets. Emily had been averse to publication. It was as foreign to her thought, she told Higginson, "as Firmament to Fin." Publication, she wrote in a poem (709), is "the Auction/ Of the Mind of Man." In a letter to Higginson in 1862 she wrote: "If fame belonged to me, I could not escape her — if she did not, the longest day would pass me on the chase." But Lavinia determined to show that fame belonged to her sister. Susan Dickinson was approached, without success; then Higginson was asked to edit the material; finally Mabel Loomis Todd, wife of a professor at Amherst College, agreed to work on the manuscripts. Higginson had undertaken to look over the poems if they could be shown to him in fair copies; Mrs. Todd would do the heavy work first. Collaborating, they eventually published *Poems by Emily Dickinson* (1890), a selection of 116 poems. By herself, Mrs. Todd edited a selection of Emily Dickinson's letters in 1894. In 1896, however, a quarrel broke out between Lavinia and Mrs. Todd; the first result was that Emily Dickinson's manuscripts were divided. The papers in Lavinia's possession passed to Susan Dickinson, and subsequently to Martha Dickinson Bianchi, Emily's niece. From 1914 until her death in 1943, Mrs. Bianchi issued several volumes of Emily Dickinson's poems. But Mrs. Todd's share of the manuscripts remained under lock until her daughter, Millicent Todd Bingham, published about 650 unpublished poems as *Bolts of Melody* (1945). Finally, Thomas H. Johnson brought all the known poems together in *The Poems of Emily Dickinson* (1955), in three volumes, giving all the available poems and their variant readings. *The Letters of Emily Dickinson*, edited by Mr. Johnson and Theodora Ward, was published in three volumes in 1958. Mr. Johnson has also published *The Complete Poems of Emily Dickinson* in one volume (1960) and a rich sample called *Final Harvest: Emily Dickinson's Poems* (1961), a selection in paperback of her choice work, 576 poems from the 1775 of the variorum edition.

Appropriately, Mr. Johnson's work on the manuscripts has been greatly praised. Before 1955, it was impossible to know precisely what authority the printed volumes had. It was feared that the early editors had been more zealous than scrupulous; they had a difficult, angular poet on their hands, so perhaps they had smoothed the rough patches. In fact, they compromised, retaining the exact text when it was tolerably lucid and altering a word or two when the poet ran beyond that mark. Not very many poems are seriously affected. "Further in Summer than the Birds" (1068) was smoothed by Higginson's hand, the third stanza made to follow a more conventional grammar than that given in the original version. There are some readers, including Yvor Winters, who prefer the smooth version; they met Emily Dickinson's poems for the first time in the old editions, and they resent the modern scholar's insistence upon textual fidelity, if it means revising old affections. The same readers, long accustomed to the conventional punctuation of the old editions, cannot welcome the dashes, Emily Dickinson's favorite gesture, reproduced in the Johnson edition. It has been argued that the dashes are rhetorical rather than grammatical notes, hints to the reading voice rather than to the silent eye. There is also the problem of the capitals: not every noun in the manuscripts is awarded a capital, but a method is dimly visible. In most cases the capitalized words are those upon which the fate of the line largely depends, so it is natural that the poet should wish to give them a mark of special favor, "italicized, as 'twere." The words thus appraised begin to look and sound like moral universals; as if they were more than nouns. Again, many of the best poems exist in different versions; the poet often incorporated them in letters, and she felt inclined to tinker with them, perhaps in deference to their recipients. Mr. Johnson is reasonably sure, in the crucial poems, how the sequence of the manuscripts goes. In some instances the versions are sufficiently distinct to make separate poems. Where choice is obligatory, Mr. Johnson has nearly always chosen well. But the procedure is doubtful in one respect; as a general policy, later texts are preferred, but in some cases the later version spoils the poem. There are two copies of "I Years had been from Home" (609) and it is possible to think the earlier version of 1862 the better poem, more powerful than the official version of 1872. Logically, Mr. Johnson's policy gives preference to the later poem, so this is the only one offered in *Final Harvest*. On the other hand, Mr. Johnson has chosen the earlier version of "The Moon upon her fluent Route" (1528) for sound poetic reasons. The result is a certain confusion between editorial principle in the selection of copy texts and a natural desire to see Emily Dickinson represented by her best poems. In some cases a satisfactory choice cannot be made. "Essential Oils — are wrung" (675) exists in two versions, their implications mutually incompatible, one hopeful, one despairing. Both were written about the same time. Mr. Johnson has given the hopeful one his preference, so it stands in *Final Harvest*; the despairing voice can only be heard in small print in the variorum edition.

But these are minor troubles, hardly to be counted at all in the great satisfaction: the extraordinary body of poetry is available. Readers make their own anthologies, the choice poems brought to memory. There are readers who love the comic poems, which I have not mentioned; Emily Dickinson's wit was not continuous, but it was strong when it appeared. There are other readers who care for the quirky poems, sardonic glances at eternal verities. Emily Dickinson was often irreverent; some readers are attracted by her boldness. In "God is a distant — stately Lover" (357) Christ's coming on earth in behalf of the Father is compared to

43

John Alden's service in behalf of Miles Standish in Longfellow's poem. Rev. Brooke Herford read the verses in the Boston *Christian Register* and thought them "one of the most offensive bits of contemptuous Unitarianism that I have met with." The editor of the *Register* disagreed, and wrote an editorial to defend the poet. But Emily Dickinson's transaction with God is a longer story.

If I admit a bias, it is in favor of those poems in which Emily Dickinson's sensibility encounters the great moral universals: love, pain, loss, doubt, death. What happens to the universals, what happens to the sensibility: the poems which give this double drama are among the greatest poems in the language. R. P. Blackmur said that in Emily Dickinson "direct experience (often invented, sometimes originally contingent) was always for the sake of something else which would replace the habit and the destructive gusto (but not the need) of experience in the world, and become an experience of its own on its own warrant and across a safe or forbidding gap." The gap is visible, or nearly visible, in the letters. The "something else" for which Emily Dickinson lived is in the poems, unless we say, with no more ado, that it is the poems themselves, poetry. The something else may be fulfilled in the poetry, with no remainder; or the poetry may be an instrument, means to a further end on the other side of silence. Between such alternatives it is hardly necessary to make a choice.

⤳ Selected Bibliography

Poems of Emily Dickinson

Poems of Emily Dickinson, edited by Mabel Loomis Todd and T. W. Higginson. Boston: Roberts Brothers, 1890.

Poems by Emily Dickinson, Second Series, edited by Mabel Loomis Todd and T. W. Higginson. Boston: Roberts Brothers, 1891.

Poems by Emily Dickinson, Third Series, edited by Mabel Loomis Todd. Boston: Roberts Brothers, 1896.

The Single Hound, edited by Martha Dickinson Bianchi. Boston: Little, Brown, 1914.

The Complete Poems of Emily Dickinson, edited by Martha Dickinson Bianchi and Alfred Leete Hampson. Boston: Little, Brown, 1924.

Further Poems of Emily Dickinson, edited by Martha Dickinson Bianchi and Alfred Leete Hampson. Boston: Little, Brown, 1929.

The Poems of Emily Dickinson, edited by Martha Dickinson Bianchi and Alfred Leete Hampson. Boston: Little, Brown, 1930.

Unpublished Poems of Emily Dickinson, edited by Martha Dickinson Bianchi and Alfred Leete Hampson. Boston: Little, Brown, 1935.

Poems by Emily Dickinson, edited by Martha Dickinson Bianchi and Alfred Leete Hampson. Boston: Little, Brown, 1937.

Ancestors' Brocades: The Literary Debut of Emily Dickinson by Millicent Todd Bingham. New York: Harper, 1945. (Contains some poems and letters published for the first time.)

Bolts of Melody: New Poems of Emily Dickinson, edited by Mabel Loomis Todd and Millicent Todd Bingham. New York: Harper, 1945.

The Poems of Emily Dickinson, edited by Thomas H. Johnson. 3 vols. Cambridge, Mass.: Harvard University Press, 1955.

The Complete Poems of Emily Dickinson, edited by Thomas H. Johnson. Boston: Little, Brown, 1960.

Final Harvest: Emily Dickinson's Poems, edited by Thomas H. Johnson. Boston: Little, Brown, 1961.

Letters of Emily Dickinson

The Letters of Emily Dickinson, edited by Mabel Loomis Todd. 2 vols. Boston: Roberts Brothers, 1894.

The Life and Letters of Emily Dickinson, edited by Martha Dickinson Bianchi. Boston: Houghton Mifflin, 1924.

Letters of Emily Dickinson, edited by Mabel Loomis Todd. New York: Harper, 1931.

Emily Dickinson Face to Face: Unpublished Letters with Notes and Reminiscences, edited by Martha Dickinson Bianchi. Boston: Houghton Mifflin, 1932.

Emily Dickinson's Letters to Dr. and Mrs. Josiah Gilbert Holland, edited by Theodora Van Wagenen Ward. Cambridge, Mass.: Harvard University Press, 1951.

Emily Dickinson: A Revelation, by Millicent Todd Bingham. New York: Harper, 1954. (Contains letters published for the first time.)

The Letters of Emily Dickinson, edited by Thomas H. Johnson and Theodora Ward. 3 vols. Cambridge, Mass.: Harvard University Press, 1958.

The Years and Hours of Emily Dickinson, edited by Jay Leyda. 2 vols. New Haven, Conn.: Yale University Press, 1960.

Concordance

Rosenbaum, S. P., editor. *A Concordance to the Poems of Emily Dickinson.* Ithaca, N.Y.: Cornell University Press, 1964.

Biographical Studies

Higgins, David. *Portrait of Emily Dickinson: The Poet and Her Prose.* New Brunswick, N.J.: Rutgers University Press, 1967.

Johnson, Thomas H. *Emily Dickinson: An Interpretive Biography.* Cambridge, Mass.: Harvard University Press, 1955.

Ward, Theodora. *The Capsule of the Mind: Chapters in the Life of Emily Dickinson.* Cambridge, Mass.: Harvard University Press, 1961.

Whicher, George F. *This Was a Poet: A Critical Biography of Emily Dickinson.* New York: Scribner's, 1938.

Critical Studies

Anderson, Charles R. *Emily Dickinson's Poetry: Stairway of Surprise.* New York: Holt, Rinehart and Winston, 1960.

Blackmur, R. P. *Language as Gesture.* New York: Harcourt, Brace, 1952.

————. "Emily Dickinson's Notation," *Kenyon Review,* 18:224–37 (Spring 1956).

Cambon, Glauco. "Emily Dickinson and the Crisis of Self-Reliance," in Myron Simon and Thornton H. Parsons, editors, *Transcendentalism and Its Legacy.* Ann Arbor: University of Michigan Press, 1966.

Capps, Jack L. *Emily Dickinson's Reading 1836–1886.* Cambridge, Mass.: Harvard University Press, 1966.

Chase, Richard. *Emily Dickinson.* New York: William Sloane Associates, 1951.

Donoghue, Denis. *Connoisseurs of Chaos.* New York: Macmillan, 1965.

Franklin, R. W. *The Editing of Emily Dickinson: A Reconsideration.* Madison: University of Wisconsin Press, 1967.

Frye, Northrop. *Fables of Identity.* New York: Harcourt, Brace and World, 1963.

Gelpi, Albert J. *Emily Dickinson: The Mind of the Poet.* Cambridge, Mass.: Harvard University Press, 1965.

Griffith, Clark. *The Long Shadow: Emily Dickinson's Tragic Poetry.* Princeton, N.J.: Princeton University Press, 1964.

Pearce, Roy Harvey. *The Continuity of American Poetry.* Princeton, N.J.: Princeton University Press, 1961.

Poulet, Georges. *Studies in Human Time,* translated by Elliott Coleman. Baltimore: Johns Hopkins Press, 1956.

Ransom, John Crowe. "Emily Dickinson: A Poet Restored," *Perspectives USA,* 15:5–20 (Spring 1956).

Tate, Allen. *Collected Essays.* Denver: Alan Swallow, 1959.

Warren, Austin. "Emily Dickinson," *Sewanee Review,* 65:565–86 (Autumn 1957).

Wells, Henry W. *Introduction to Emily Dickinson.* Chicago: Packard, 1947.

Winters, Yvor. *Maule's Curse.* Norfolk, Conn.: New Directions, 1938.

_____. *Forms of Discovery.* Denver: Alan Swallow, 1967.

PS1541
Z5D6

A 5064

Donoghue, Denis.
    Emily Dickinson. Minneapolis, University of Minn
Press ₁1969₁

    47 p. 21 cm. (University of Minnesota pamphlets on An
writers, no. 81) 0.95

    Bibliography: p. 45–47.   8 12/07

    1. Dickinson, Emily, 1830–1886. I. Series: Minnesota. Uni
Pamphlets on American writers, no. 81

    PS1541.Z5D6   811'.4   76–(

    Library of Congress   70 ₁7₁